fun with crewel embroidery

fun with crewel

embroidery

by erica wilson

ILLUSTRATED WITH PHOTOGRAPHS AND DRAWINGS

charles scribner's sons NEW YORK

ACKNOWLEDGMENTS

The designs for the tittlemice embroidery shown on pages 1, 2, 3, 34, and 35 were inspired by *The Tale of Mrs. Tittlemouse* by Beatrix Potter, published by Frederick Warne & Co., London. Reproduced by permission of the publishers and of the Honourable Mrs. A. E. Pleydell-Bouverie who worked the embroidery.

The sampler worked by Ann Dowie, aged 10, 1798, pictured on page 6 is reproduced by permission of the Metropolitan Museum of Art, Gift of Katherine de B. Parsons and her brother Livingston Parsons, 1941.

Photographs of the following designs by Erica Wilson are reproduced through the courtesy of young embroideresses:

    Fish eyeglass cases, page 10—Lorraine Helen Froeb (6) and Elise Lynch (9)
    Bird pillow, page 16—Jessica Kagan (5)
    Mushroom pillow, page 20—Julie Kirkham (10)
    Butterfly pillow, page 21—Sara Kirkham (9)
    Squirrel pillow, page 21—Charlotte Matteson (10)
    Sampler, page 25—Elise Lynch (10)
    Elephant, page 28—Anne Thatcher (7)

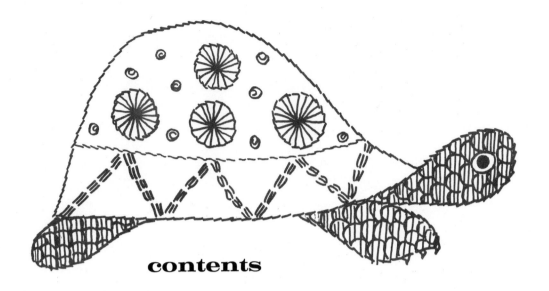

contents

7   Introduction

8   Materials You Will Need

11 A Bag

14 A Fish Eyeglass Case

17 A Bird Pillow

19 Transferring Designs

23 A Toaster Cover

25 A Sampler

27 The Moonflower Design

28 An Elephant

29 Enlarging Designs

31 A Mouse Pillow

33 A Cat Pillow

35 The Tittlemice

36 A Sentry

39 A Sun Rug

41 Alphabet of Stitches

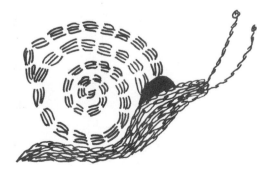

A sampler worked in Cross Stitch in 1798 by Ann Dowie, aged 10

The author's first piece of embroidery, designed and worked at age 5½

introduction

Long ago in England the name for a ball of wool thread was Clew, and later Cruell. That is why today, when we talk of Crewel Embroidery we mean stitching with wool on fabric. Crewel embroidery was done by the Stuart Queens of England, and was used by the early American settlers to decorate their beds, ornament their pocketbooks or even to beautify their petticoats.

Traditionally, it was done with very fine wool on linen, but you can find a piece of tweed and work with heavy rug yarn, or use mending wool on denim or pillow ticking. In my first piece of embroidery, which you see on the opposite page, I used scraps of my aunt's needlepoint wool and worked on organdy as it was the only material I had. The fun of the whole thing is using different stitches and exciting colors. You can *paint* with your needle anything from a lion to a ladybug, and *make* anything from a belt to a bedspread.

A petticoat border worked by an American colonist in the 18th century

FABRICS   Choose your fabric first. You can use all kinds of materials as long as they have a fairly open weave. Linen wears best for chair seats; a firm denim, striped like ticking, comes in gay colors perfect for an apron or belt; the texture of burlap is ideal for a rug or wall hanging.

WOOLS   Use heavy crewel yarn several threads thick for coarse-weave linens and denim, fine English crewel yarn for more closely woven fabrics. The thickness of wool depends on the fabric you have selected. Three or four strands of fine wool may be substituted for one strand of heavy wool but there is no good substitute for rug wool.

NEEDLES   The most useful needles are a rug needle, tapestry needle No. 18, chenille needle No. 18 and crewel needle No. 3. Remember, the higher the number, the finer the needle. You can use almost any size, providing the needle makes a large enough hole to protect the wool as you pull it through the fabric, and has a long eye so that it can be threaded easily.

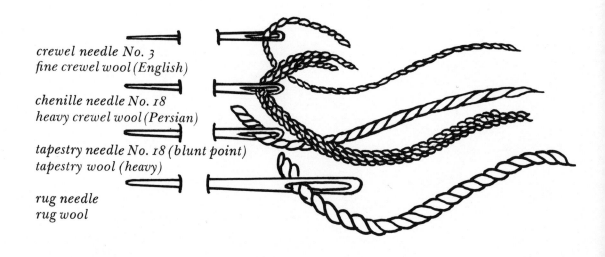

crewel needle No. 3
fine crewel wool (English)

chenille needle No. 18
heavy crewel wool (Persian)

tapestry needle No. 18 (blunt point)
tapestry wool (heavy)

rug needle
rug wool

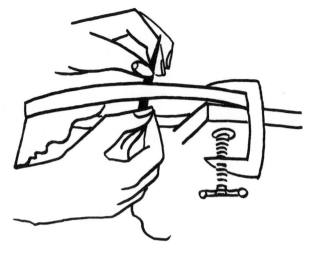

hand frame with "C" clamp

floor frame

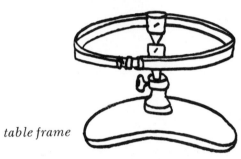

table frame

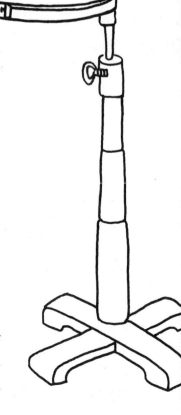

FRAMES A frame is most important. It will make your work easy to do and the finished results smooth and even. The frame should be wood, not metal, so that it does not slip, and should have an adjusting screw, so that you can make the fabric as tight as a drum. It should have a support (like the ones shown above). This leaves both your hands free for working, one below and one above the frame. Or you can buy a hand hoop and fasten it to the table with a "C" clamp from any hardware store. The drawing illustrating the "C" clamp also shows how all frames should be used.

To stitch, stab the needle up and down, keeping one hand *always underneath* and the other *always on top* of the fabric in the frame. After a little practice you will be able to work with great speed.

Making a colorful bag or an eyeglass case shaped like a fish in needle-point canvas is the easiest way to learn crewel embroidery.

MATERIALS   *½ yd. "single thread" needlepoint canvas,*
            12, 14, or 16 threads to the inch
            tapestry needle No. 18
            scraps of wool of any kind

To make this bag, first measure a rectangle 6″ x 18″ on your canvas, leaving a 4-inch border on all sides for turnings. Draw the shape by guiding a pencil between the threads of the canvas. This rectangle will later be folded in half and stitched together to form the bag.

Now stretch the canvas in your frame. Thread the needle with a strand of wool about 18 inches long. Knot one end, and you are ready to begin stitching.

THREADING THE NEEDLE

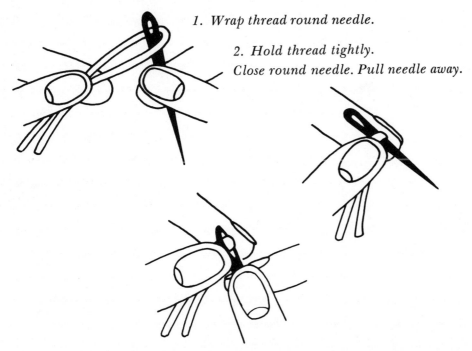

1. Wrap thread round needle.

2. Hold thread tightly.
Close round needle. Pull needle away.

3. Squeeze thread tightly between finger and thumb. Press eye of needle down onto thread. Pull thread through eye from top of needle.

12   Stab the needle up at one edge of your bag; work lines back and forth across the 6-inch width of the rectangle. You can jump *over* as many threads of the canvas as you want, but always go *under* only one. This leaves most of the wool on the surface. Be sure to use enough strands of yarn in the needle to cover the canvas well. Make regular patterns by counting the threads of the canvas, as shown below, or make a random pattern without counting at all. End off your threads by sewing into the small stitches on the back.

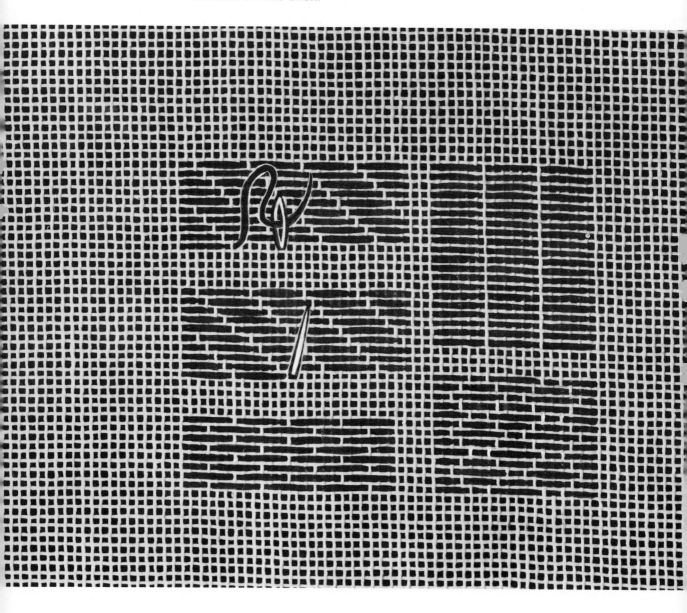

BUTTONHOLE STITCH FOR EDGING

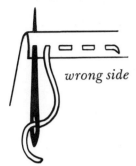

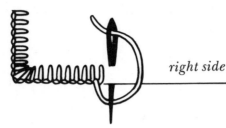

1. To start, take several stitches into the hem, come out at the left corner.

wrong side

right side

2. Working from left to right, take a stitch about ¼" long between each thread of the canvas. Loop thread under needle as shown.

3. To join thread invisibly, always come up inside the last loop and begin stitching.

4. "Oversew" the loops together as shown. Pull stitches firm.

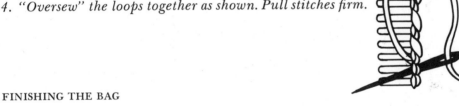

FINISHING THE BAG

Trim your finished embroidery leaving ½-inch turnings. Crease the turnings to the reverse side and buttonhole stitch the bag all around, as illustrated above. Then fold it in half and sew both sides together, oversewing through the loops formed by the buttonhole stitches as shown in drawing 4. Finally, make a thick wool braid for a handle, knot it at either end and sew it to the bag. See photograph on page 10.

To make a braid, knot a bundle of threads together at one end. Secure the knotted end to any firm object. Divide the bundle into three equal sections. Bring the left section over the middle one to the center, then the right group over that to the center. Keep repeating this process until you have a braid long enough for the handle of your handbag, and end it with a knot.

BRAID

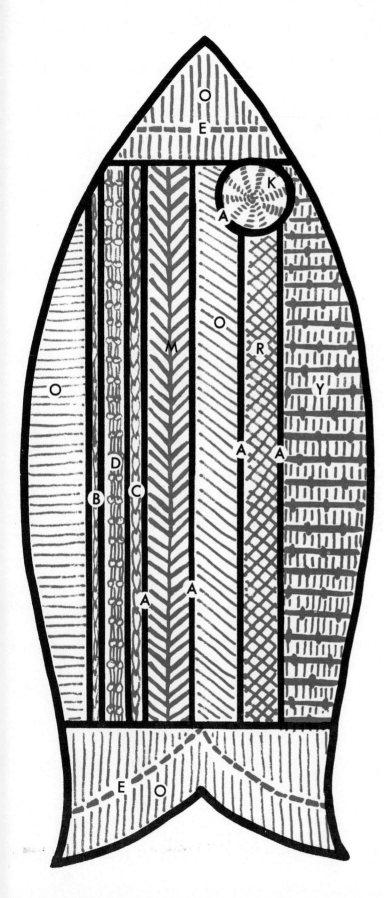

making a fish eyeglass case

MATERIALS   *¼ yd. needlepoint canvas, 14 threads to the inch*
tapestry needle No. 18
heavy crewel or tapestry wool in three or four colors
¼ yd. colored felt

If you lay a piece of needlepoint canvas over this page, you will find the dark outlines of the drawing show through distinctly, so that you can easily trace the fish onto the canvas with a soft pencil or a felt-tipped water color pen, which you can buy at most stationery stores. Keep the canvas threads parallel with the straight lines of the fish pattern, as you trace. Then put the work in a frame. Now you are ready to learn real crewel stitches.

In the drawing the stitches are shown in a lighter shade. Each is labeled with a letter. Look in the stitch alphabet starting on page 41 for all stitch instructions.

FISH STITCHES

A	STEM	**K**	SPIDER'S WEB *whipped*
B	SPLIT	**M**	FISHBONE
C	CHAIN	**O**	SATIN
D	COUCHING	**R**	CLOSE HERRINGBONE
E	BACK	**Y**	LAID WORK

Begin your thread with a knot and end by stitching into the back of the fish, as you did with the bag. Satin Stitch (**O**) the entire nose and tail, then work the Back Stitch (**E**) over the top afterwards. Work long Laid Work stitches (**Y**) from head to tail. Sew them down with stitches worked straight across on top.

FINISHING THE FISH

Cut out the fish, leaving ½-inch turnings on the canvas all around. Cut snips into these turnings so that you can fold them back easily. Iron them down, using a damp cloth, so that they lie flat. Now cut two fish shapes, the exact size of the pattern, out of felt. Sew one felt piece to the back of your fish as a lining using the same small oversewing stitch you learned in finishing the bag on page 13. Then attach the second piece of felt in the same way, as an outside back, leaving the tail open so that the glasses will slip in easily.

Edge the fish all around with a cord to cover your stitching. To make a cord, knot two single lengths of wool together at each end. Secure one end to any firm object. Insert a pencil at the other end (see diagram) and turn it to twist the wool until you have a single tightly twisted length of wool. Then fold it in half, allow the wool to twist back on itself into a nice thick cord, stroke it smooth and knot the open end. With a single strand of the same wool, stitch the cord to the edge of the fish with slanted stitches which conceal themselves in the rope.

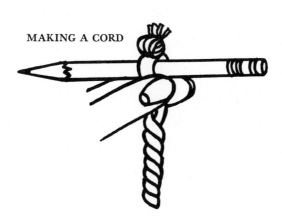

MAKING A CORD

making a bird pillow

MATERIALS ½ yd. coarse linen
heavy crewel wool in five bright colors
chenille needle No. 18
tapestry needle No. 18
velvet welting in contrasting color
pillow filler, 14" diameter

Now that you have learned to do crewel stitches on canvas you are ready to try them on other fabrics. On page 18 you will find the design for the bird pillow drawn to its exact size.

Trace the birds and berries on heavy tracing paper, cut them out and pin them to your linen so that they form an attractive design within a 14 inch diameter circle. Now connect them with branches which you can draw freehand. You may want to copy the pillow in the photograph or you may prefer to make your own arrangement. Then draw around the paper patterns with a felt-tipped water color pen. When you unpin your patterns, your design will be clearly outlined, all ready for working. Always leave plenty of material around your design so that you can put the fabric into the frame easily. Cut it to shape only after your embroidery is finished.

Follow the chart on the following page and the stitch alphabet beginning on page 41 for the stitch instructions. Use a chenille needle and one strand of heavy crewel yarn. A tapestry needle is useful for weaving the Spider's Webs (K) as its blunt point slides under the threads instead of piercing them.

The pillow on the jacket has a velvet welting all around, making a contrasting color "frame" to the design. Alternatively, pillows can be backed with contrasting fabric such as velvet, or edged with a cord like the one you used to edge the fish on page 15. You will see other ideas for pillows on the following pages.

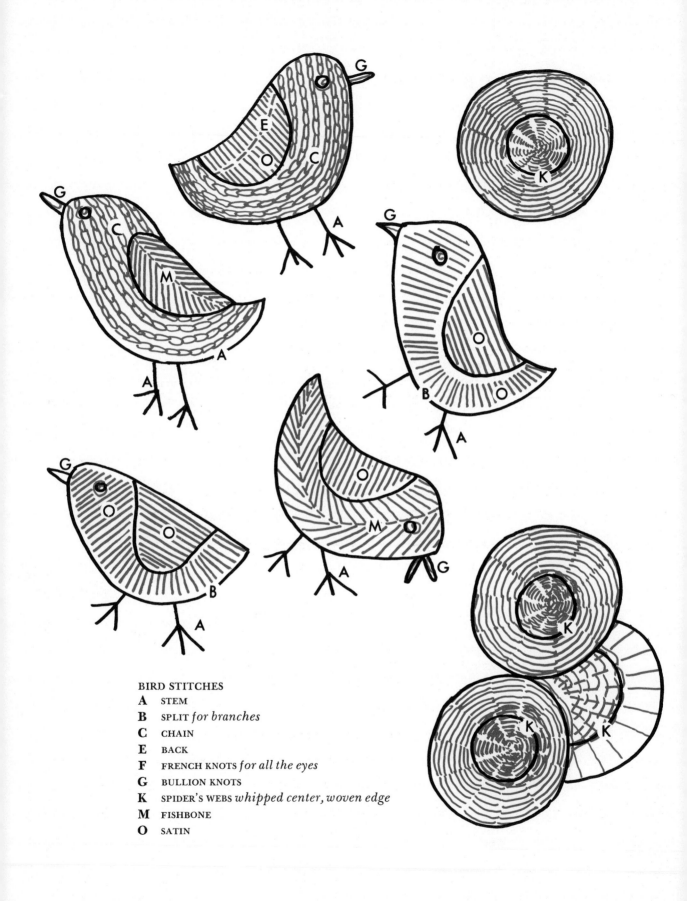

BIRD STITCHES
A STEM
B SPLIT *for branches*
C CHAIN
E BACK
F FRENCH KNOTS *for all the eyes*
G BULLION KNOTS
K SPIDER'S WEBS *whipped center, woven edge*
M FISHBONE
O SATIN

The following motifs can all be traced and worked like the bird pillow you have just finished. Some of the shapes, though, are a little too detailed to cut out and trace around as you did with the bird pillow so you will find it easier to transfer them to the material in one of the following ways. First, trace the design onto heavy tracing paper using a soft pencil so that you don't damage your book. Then, choose whichever method is right for your material.

1 DRESSMAKERS' CARBON—For light-colored fabrics. Dressmakers' carbon is available in notions departments of most stores. Use only the dark blue as the other colors won't show clearly. (Caution: never use typewriter carbon—it will smudge.) Secure your fabric with masking tape to any hard flat surface. Center your paper pattern on top of the material and slide the carbon, face downwards, between the design and the fabric. To prevent the pattern from slipping, weight it down with some books. Then trace firmly over the design, using a slightly blunt pencil so as not to tear the paper. Lift a corner of the design occasionally to make sure it is transferring well. If it is not, press harder, and go over the lines again.

2 TRANSFER PENCIL—For dark-colored fabrics. A pink transfer pencil, which you can buy in notions departments, is useful for darker fabrics which won't show carbon. Draw over the lines on the back of your tracing with it, then iron this pattern, pink side down, onto the material. The iron should be fairly hot to get a good impression so be careful not to scorch the fabric.

BUTTERFLY STITCHES
A STEM
B SPLIT
C CHAIN
F FRENCH KNOTS
K SPIDER'S WEBS *whipped*
M FISHBONE
O SATIN

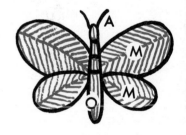

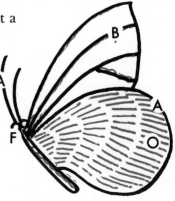

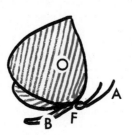

When you work on tweed or any fabric with a very rough surface, the first two methods may not work well. In this case draw your design onto the material freehand with blackboard chalk, and then go over it with a felt-tipped water color pen, to make it more permanent.

The stitches used in the motifs are drawn inside the shapes in a lighter shade. Refer to the drawings for the stitches you will need and find the instructions for them in the stitch alphabet on page 41.

Of course you can use your own ideas not only for the stitches but also for the arrangement of the patterns. For instance, the butterflies on page 19 might be used to decorate a belt or an apron, or combined with the squirrel for a chair seat, or arranged to make a small round pillow, as shown opposite.

F FRENCH KNOTS
G BULLION KNOTS
I SEEDING
M FISHBONE
T RAISED STEM
W BURDEN
Y LAID WORK

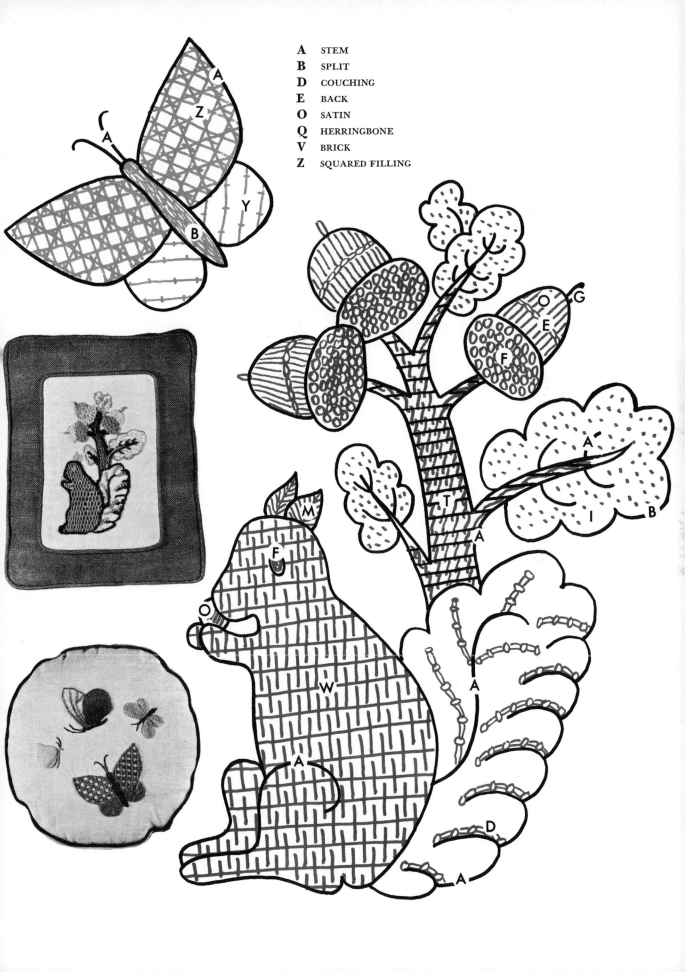

A STEM
B SPLIT
D COUCHING
E BACK
O SATIN
Q HERRINGBONE
V BRICK
Z SQUARED FILLING

MATERIALS *½ yd. ticking or striped denim*
1 packet binding tape

or buy a plain ready-made toaster cover in any fabric

9" squares of felt in four or five colors
any scraps of wool matching the felt

The rooster on this gay toaster cover was cut out in bright red felt and then sewn to red and white ticking with wool French Knots. This idea can be applied with equal success to many of the designs shown in this book. For instance, a sweater, skirt or apron could be decorated with the bright butterflies and mushrooms shown on pages 19 to 21. The contrasting colored French Knots add greatly to the decorative effect and hold the design in place.

TO EMBROIDER THE TOASTER COVER—Trace the rooster onto the felt, using the transferring instructions on page 19. Cut him out and pin him to the ticking. Next cut out a series of circles in contrasting colors and pin them to the rooster. Sew these polka dots down firmly with French Knots using one strand of wool. Secure the tail, feet and crest with more French Knots and work a Bullion Knot for the beak. For the instructions for French and Bullion Knots, see letters **F** and **G** in the stitch alphabet beginning on page 41.

TO MAKE UP THE TOASTER COVER—Since toasters vary in size and shape, cut out a paper pattern, pin it together and try it on your toaster. When you have a good fit, cut the ticking from this pattern. Then sew it together, using binding tape to edge it.

ABC^A

making a sampler

MATERIALS *½ yd. firmly woven light color striped denim, 36" wide*
fine crewel wool
chenille needle No. 18
crewel needle No. 3
tapestry needle No. 18

This sampler includes most of the stitches in the book and is a good way to practice them. It is worked on pink-and-white denim with the stripes running horizontally, which is helpful for arranging the motifs on straight lines. Finished measurements are 9" x 26½".

Follow the chart on the opposite page and the instructions in the alphabet of stitches beginning on page 41. Experiment by using your own stitches and arrange the design as you please, using fine crewel yarn both single and double to give variety of texture. For instance, the Herringbone (**Q**) on the roof must be single strand to give a lacy effect, but the Whipped and Woven Spider's Webs (**K**) look best when two strands are used. Make all the eyes in French Knots (**F**) and cut the Turkey Work (**U**) flowers to look like pompoms. The bands across, reading from top to bottom, are worked in Couching (**D**) outlined with Stem Stitch (**A**); Vandyke (**S**); Chain (**C**); Couching (**D**); Roumanian (**N**).

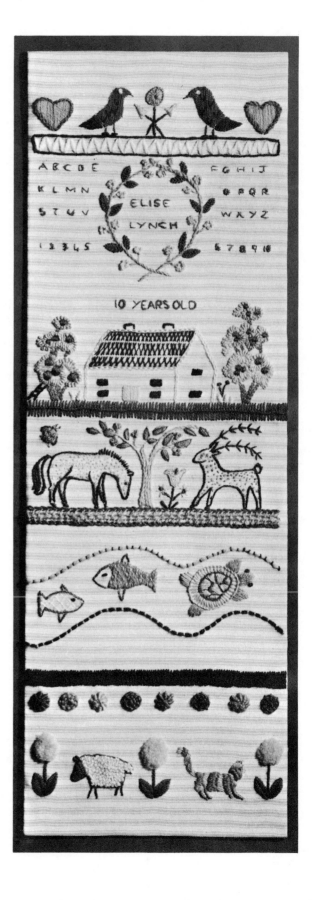

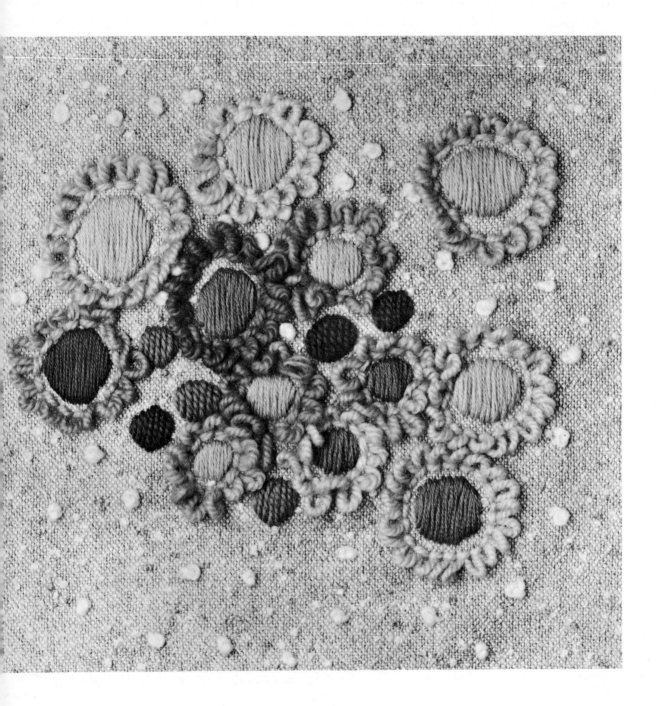

"Moonflowers" are designs made simply by arranging different-sized circles to fill a square. Several may be mounted as a wall panel, as shown here. Many may be joined to form a bedspread, or applied to a ready-made one. Single squares might be used as stool tops, or would make beautiful gift pillows.

MATERIALS *open-weave fabric (rayon-and-cotton mixture with*
rough linen effect is used here)
each square measures 18" x 18"
rug wool
heavy crewel wool
rug needle
tapestry needle No. 18

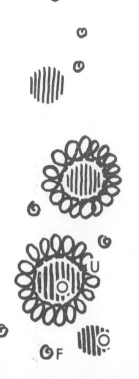

Using a fine felt-tipped water color pen, trace around any circular shape from a fifty-cent piece to a dinner plate, arranging the circles in different sizes as you see them here.

Follow the charts below and find the stitch instructions in the stitch alphabet beginning on page 41. Turkey Work, uncut, (**U**), French Knots (**F**) and Satin Stitch (**O**) are done in rug yarn while 2 threads of heavy crewel wool are used for Chain Stitch (**C**), Roumanian Stitch (**N**), Stem Stitch (**A**) and Whipped Spider's Webs (**K**). You might use a gay color scheme of bright pink, peach and yellow on natural linen—too many colors will spoil the simplicity of the design.

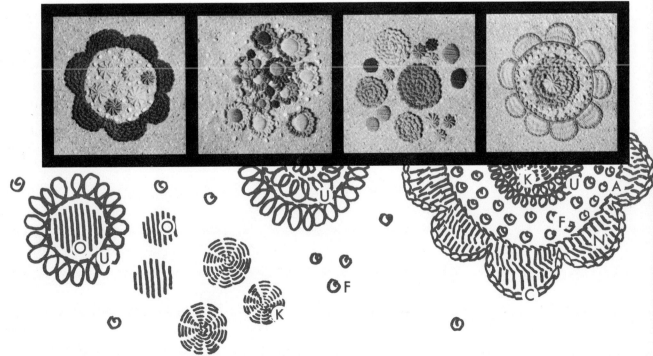

*This elephant is worked on gray tweed in Stem Stitch (**A**) using white rug wool. He stands in a jungle of lime-green Fishbone-Stitch leaves (**M**). He will make a good-sized pillow to throw on the floor as an extra seat for a friend, a carry-all bag, or a wall panel.*

The illustration below shows how to enlarge a design by using squares. To enlarge the elephant and the designs on the following pages, draw a rectangle on tracing paper to the size given with each pattern.

TO ENLARGE THE ELEPHANT—Draw a rectangle 18″ x 16″. Cut it out and fold it in half four times. When you open it up you will have 16 large squares, exactly as in the drawing below but proportionately larger. With a pencil, rule the lines of the folds, so that you can see them clearly. Now draw the elephant shape within these large squares, making sure the lines cross the squares at exactly the same points as in the small drawing on this page.

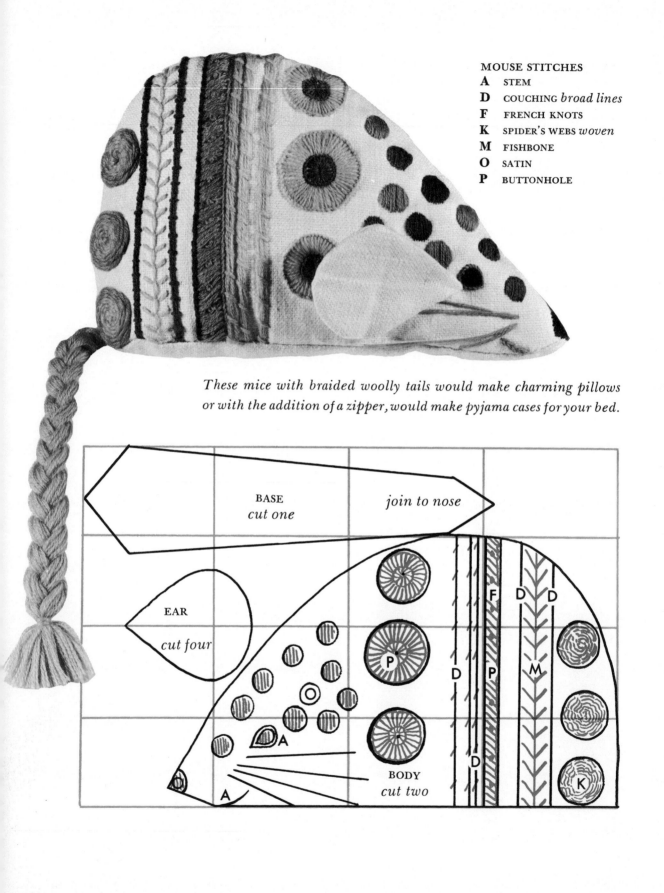

MOUSE STITCHES

A	STEM
D	COUCHING *broad lines*
F	FRENCH KNOTS
K	SPIDER'S WEBS *woven*
M	FISHBONE
O	SATIN
P	BUTTONHOLE

These mice with braided woolly tails would make charming pillows or with the addition of a zipper, would make pyjama cases for your bed.

BASE
cut one

join to nose

EAR

cut four

BODY
cut two

MATERIALS *½ yd. of corduroy, tweed, linen, or burlap*
heavy crewel wool, or any thick yarn
chenille needle No. 18
tapestry needle No. 18
¼ yd. crinoline or buckram, for stiffening ears
down, dacron or kapok for filling the pillow

Draw and cut out a rectangle from tracing paper 19¾" x 13" and enlarge the pattern from the opposite page, as you did with the elephant. (See page 29.) Transfer the design according to the directions given on page 19, selecting the method best suited for your material. Put the work in a frame. Do not cut your fabric to shape until the embroidery is finished.

The stitches used on the white linen mouse are marked by letters on the drawing opposite. For instructions, refer to the stitch alphabet beginning on page 41. For the whiskers, take long straight stitches. For the tail, make a thick braid 18 inches long using anything you can find—ribbon, string or wool. Follow the instructions on page 13.

FINISHING THE MOUSE

Cut out all 7 pieces of pattern leaving ½-inch turnings around each. Cut 2 ears in buckram without turnings. Sew the body together on the wrong side leaving an opening at the tail for stuffing. Turn it right side out. Stuff it with kapok or similar pillow stuffing. Insert the end of the braid into the opening you have left and sew the tail into position. Sew the ears together, leaving 2 inches open, turn them right side out, slip the buckram inside and stitch them into place.

This cat is a good companion for the mouse you have just made. She was created out of lavender tweed with orange spots and whiskers.

MATERIALS   *½ yd. of tweed, linen or coarse-textured fabric*
heavy crewel wool in about six colors
chenille needle No. 18
tapestry needle No. 18
down, dacron or kapok for filling the pillow

CAT STITCHES
A   STEM
F   FRENCH KNOTS
J   PADDED SATIN
K   SPIDER'S WEBS *woven*
M   FISHBONE
N   ROUMANIAN
O   SATIN

Make the cat in exactly the same way as the mouse pillow described on page 31. Draw and cut out two rectangles 12½" x 16" for the back and the front and one rectangle 5¾" x 10" for the feet. Enlarge the pattern from this page, using the method described on page 29. Transfer the pattern (see page 19), put the fabric in a frame, work the embroidery, cut out the 3 pieces and stitch them together. Turn right side out and stuff with kapok or similar pillow stuffing.

The stitches are shown by letters on the drawing below. For instructions, refer to the stitch alphabet beginning on page 41.

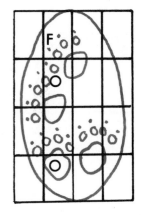

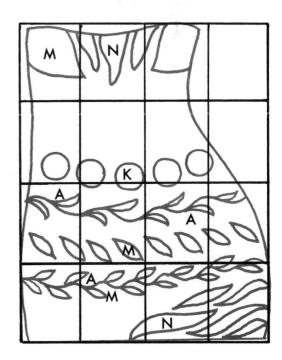

rectangle measures 10½" x 9"

rectangle measures 9½" x 10"

Mrs. Tittlemouse and friends would make attractive pillows or pictures or a charming headboard for your bed. Be sure you have tried out stitches on some of the other projects before you attempt this design.

MATERIALS   *each mouse will fit on an 18" square of*
coarse-weave white linen
fine crewel wool, using several strands
crewel needle No. 3
chenille needle No. 18

TITTLEMICE STITCHES
A   STEM
B   SPLIT
C   CHAIN
E   BACK
F   FRENCH KNOTS
G   BULLION KNOTS
H   FRENCH KNOTS ON STALKS
O   SATIN
P   BUTTONHOLE
Q   HERRINGBONE
T   RAISED STEM
U   TURKEY WORK *uncut*
Y   LAID WORK
Z   SQUARED FILLING

Draw and cut out rectangles to the size given with each mouse. Enlarge the patterns, following the method described on page 29, and transfer the designs (see page 19). Put the work in a frame. Find the instructions in the stitch alphabet at the back of the book, for the stitches shown by letters on the charts.

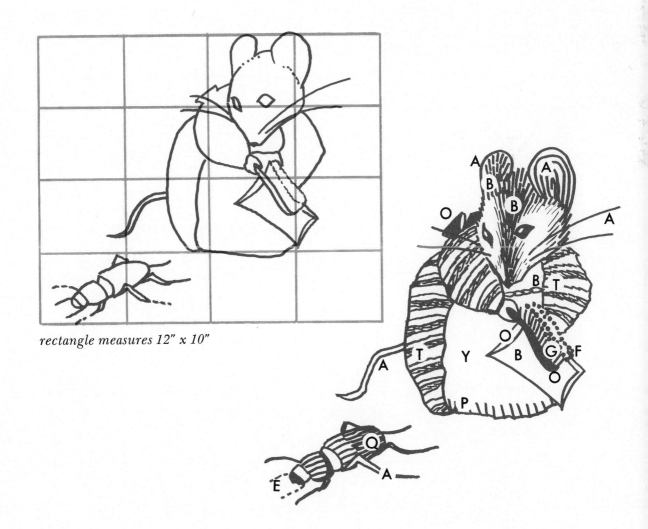

rectangle measures 12" x 10"

making a sentry

MATERIALS *1½ yd. heavy even-weave white linen or burlap rug wool rug needle*

Draw and cut out a rectangle 10½″ x 36″. Enlarge and transfer the sentry according to the instructions on pages 29 and 19. Find the instructions for the stitches shown on the chart opposite in the stitch alphabet beginning on page 41.

Use the regular weave of the material to keep your stitches straight and keep the Cross Stitch (**L**) even by counting the threads of the fabric. (The blunt point of the rug needle makes it easy to go between the threads instead of splitting them.)

As a finishing touch take long straight stitches for the sentry's cockade. Couch (**D**) his sword with heavy silver thread, the kind used for wrapping gifts. Sew it down with gray sewing thread so the stitches hardly show.

The Sentry stands boldly in red, white and blue
Guarding your toy cupboard door for you!

SENTRY STITCHES

A	STEM	**Q**	HERRINGBONE
D	COUCHING	**U**	TURKEY WORK *uncut*
L	CROSS	**V**	BRICK
O	SATIN	**X**	LAID WORK

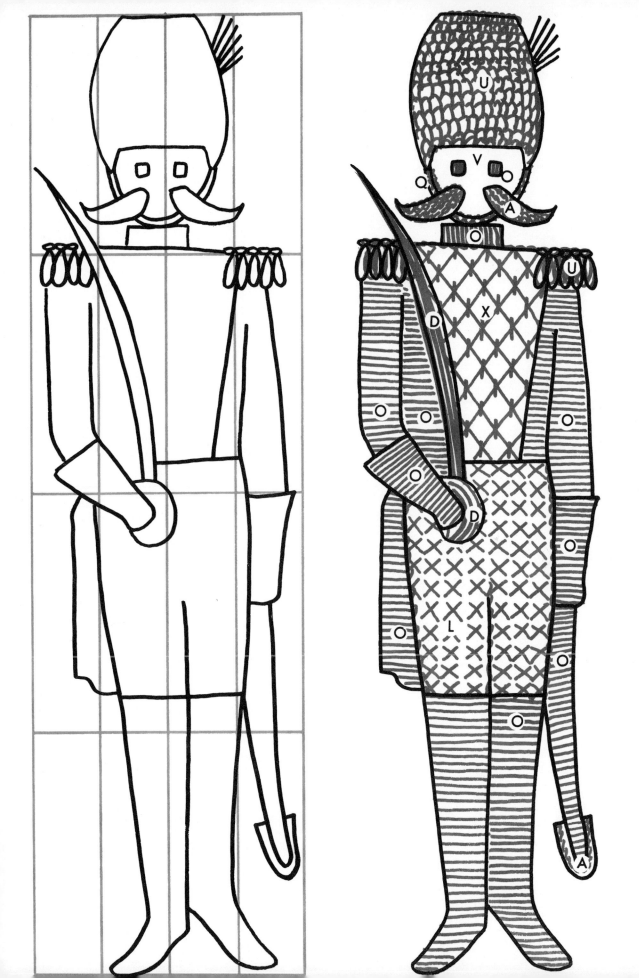

What fun to leap out of bed onto your Sun Rug in the morning! It may be embroidered on bright burlap with heavy rug yarn.

MATERIALS *1 sq. yd. burlap*
rug wool
rug needle
1 sq. yd. heavy rug weight felt

Crease the burlap in half and then in half again. On opening it you will find the exact center is marked where the two creases form a cross.

Tie one end of a piece of string approximately 24 inches long to some blackboard chalk. Ask someone to hold the other end in the center of your burlap. Shorten it to 17 inches and go around with the chalk making a 34-inch diameter circle.

Then shorten the string to 7 inches to make a 14-inch diameter circle inside the first, using the same central point. As you go along, make the design permanent by going over it with a fine felt-tipped water color pen.

In the center circle draw the face freehand, copying what you see opposite. Then draw four radiating guide lines from this circle using the original creases as guides. Next draw four more lines approximately halfway between them, and then enclose all these lines with wedge shapes as in the drawing. The wedges should be approximately 4 inches wide at the base. Finally draw freehand 5 radiating lines between these wedges. Work all the stitches according to the chart on the next page, following instructions in the stitch alphabet beginning on page 41. For the couching, sew down 4 threads with one in the needle. Leave long enough ends on this stitch to knot together and form a 3-inch tassel at the edge of the rug as in the photograph.

40

TO MAKE UP THE RUG—Cut out the burlap with a 1-inch turning all around. Make ¾-inch snips into the turning and baste it back so that the circle lies smooth and flat. Iron the rug face down into a thick blanket using a damp cloth. Now cut a perfect circle 34 inches in diameter in the felt. Using matching linen or button thread, sew the felt to the back of your rug with an oversewing stitch (see page 13).

SUN RUG STITCHES
A STEM
C CHAIN
D COUCHING
K SPIDER'S WEBS *whipped*
M FISHBONE
O SATIN
U TURKEY WORK *uncut*
W BURDEN

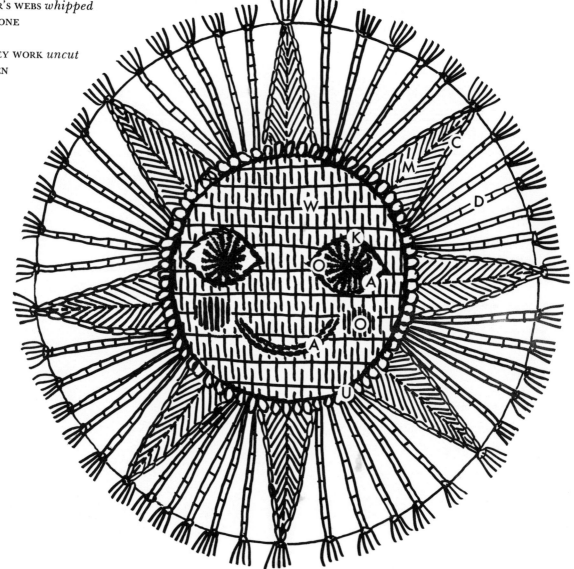

alphabet of stitches

STEM	**A**		**B**	SPLIT
CHAIN	**C**		**D**	COUCHING
			E	BACK
FRENCH KNOTS	**F**		**G**	BULLION KNOTS
FRENCH KNOTS ON STALKS	**H**		**I**	SEEDING
PADDED SATIN	**J**		**K**	SPIDER'S WEBS *whipped and woven*
			L	CROSS
FISHBONE	**M**		**N**	ROUMANIAN
SATIN	**O**		**P**	BUTTONHOLE *open and close*
HERRINGBONE	**Q**		**R**	CLOSE HERRINGBONE
			S	VANDYKE
RAISED STEM	**T**		**U**	TURKEY WORK *cut and uncut*
BRICK	**V**		**W**	BURDEN
LAID WORK *tied with criss cross*	**X**		**Y**	LAID WORK *tied with straight lines*
			Z	SQUARED FILLING

A STEM

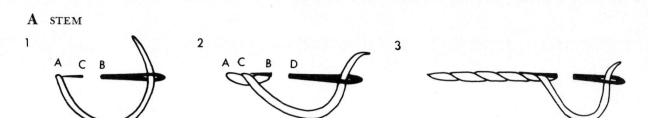

1) Come up at A, go down at B, up at C. Draw through, with thread below needle. 2) Go down at D, up at B [in the same hole]. 3) Repeat 2. Always keep thread to same side of needle.

B SPLIT

1) Come up at A, go down at B. 2) Come up from below at C, splitting right through the center of the stitch. 3) Continue in this way. This is an easy stitch to practice when learning to use both hands on the frame.

C CHAIN

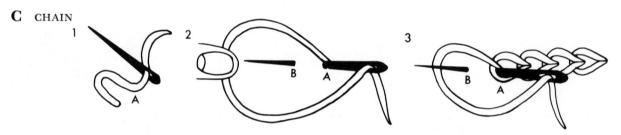

1) Come up at A. 2) Form a loop; hold it flat and return needle to the same hole at A. Come up inside loop at B and draw flat. 3) Continue, always inserting needle where thread emerges inside loop, at A.

D COUCHING

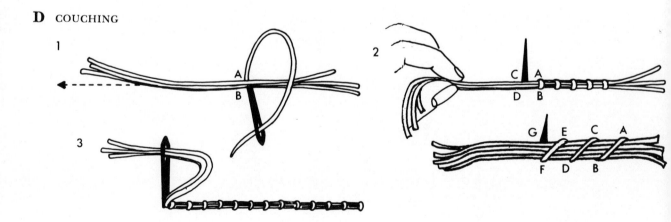

1 & 2) With one thread in needle, sew down a bundle of threads, coming up at A and going back in almost the same hole at B. [To make a smooth, broad line, sew down a fatter bundle of threads with wide *slanting* stitches.] 3) Take the ends of the bundle to the wrong side with a large needle. Cut them off ¼″ long.

E BACK

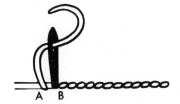

Come up at A and go down at B into the same hole as the previous stitch. Repeat, keeping all the stitches the same size.

F FRENCH KNOTS

1    2   3

1) Come up at A, twist thread once round needle. 2) Draw tight and return needle to same hole. 3) shows finished effect. [To make a fatter knot, use two or more threads.]

G BULLION KNOTS

1   2 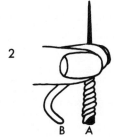   3

1) Come up at A, go down at B, leaving a loop. 2) Come up at A, and twist thread lightly several times around needle. Holding thread firmly with finger and thumb of your left hand, draw needle through with your right hand. Still holding twists firmly, draw thread tight, until the "worm" lies flat on the material. 3) Go down at the end of the twist and pull firm.

H FRENCH KNOTS ON STALKS

1 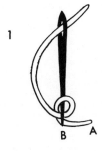   2

1) Come up at A, twist thread once round needle, draw tight and go in at B, ¼″ away from A. 2) shows finished effect.

I SEEDING

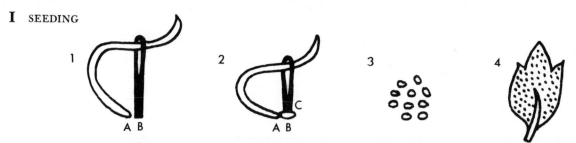

1 & 2) Take 2 little stitches on top of one another. Come up at A, go down at B, up at A, down at C. 3) Scatter stitches in any direction. 4) Leaf shows finished effect.

J PADDED SATIN

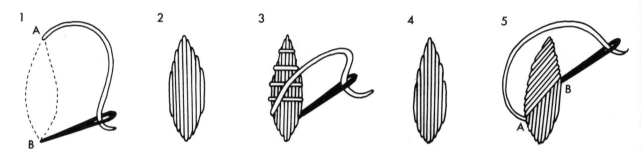

1 & 2) Starting in the center to keep stitches straight, fill shape with stitches side by side. 3) Go across with a few stitches to hold long ones flat. 4) Repeat 1 & 2. 5) Cover shape with slanting stitches. [The final stitching may be slanted or straight, depending on shape of the motif.]

K SPIDER'S WEBS *whipped and woven*

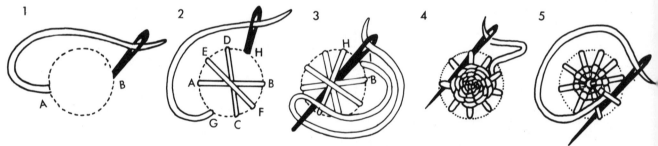

1 & 2) Make spokes across the circle [A to B, C to D, etc.]. 3) Using a blunt needle, slide it under threads where they cross. Knot threads in center by looping thread over needle, then under it. Draw upwards till tight. 4) Woven web: starting in center, weave under and over threads until all spokes are covered. 5) Whipped web: slide under 2 threads. Go back; slide under last thread taken and one new one. Continue, going back 1 and under 2 until spokes are covered.

L CROSS

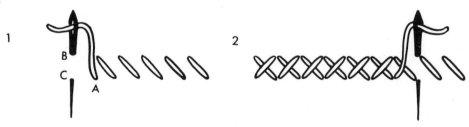

1) Working from right to left, come up at A, go down at B, up at C, directly below B. 2) Return, working from left to right into exactly the same holes. Always keep needle vertical.

M FISHBONE

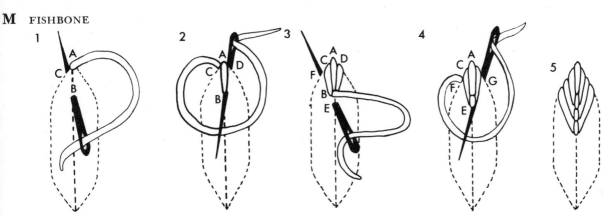

1) Come up at A, go down at B, ¼" below A. Come up at C. 2) Go in at D, loop thread under needle and come up at B, in the same hole. 3) Draw through and secure loop by going down at E, ⅛" below B. 4) Come up at F and repeat 2 & 3. Keep stitches straight down the center, by drawing a pencil guideline.

N ROUMANIAN

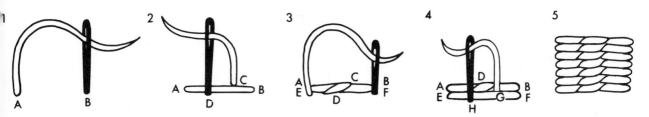

1) Come up at A, go down at B. 2) Come up at C, down at D, making a slanting stitch across the middle of the first stitch. 3 & 4) Repeat 1 & 2, from E to F, G to H. 5) Keep slanting stitches in an even line down the center as shown in 5.

O SATIN

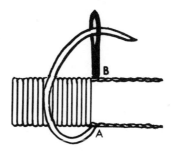

1) Come up at A, go down at B, covering shape with stitches placed neatly side by side. To assure smooth edges, first work a line of Split Stitch [**B**] on both edges, then work the Satin Stitch over this padding.

P BUTTONHOLE *open and close*

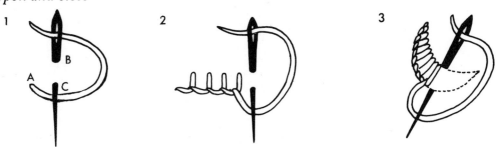

1 & 2) Work from left to right or right to left, looping thread under needle. 3) When working stitches closely, do not crowd them or they will not lie flat. [See also p. 13.]

Q HERRINGBONE

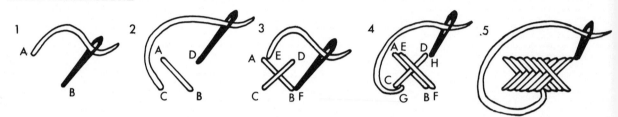

1) Come up at A, go down at B. 2) Come up at C, ¼″ behind B and level with it. Go down at D. 3) Come up at E, ¼″ behind D, and level with it. Repeat 2 & 3, making a series of overlapping cross stitches on a line. 4) shows finished effect.

R CLOSE HERRINGBONE

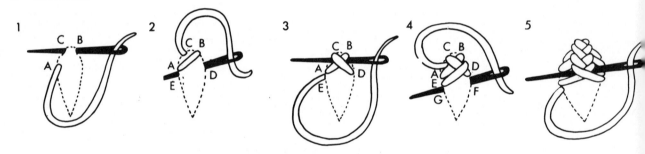

1) Come up at A, go down at B. 2) Come up at C, go down at D, forming a cross. 3 & 4) Make another cross, E to F, G to H, to the right, but touching the first. 5) Continue, making a solid band. This stitch is exactly like Herringbone [Q] but worked with closely overlapping stitches.

S VANDYKE

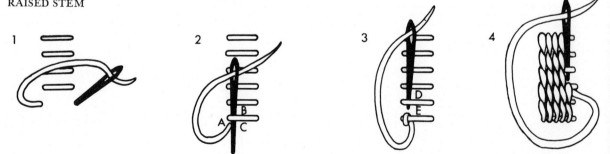

1 & 2) Using a blunt needle, make a small cross stitch, A to B, C to D. 3) Come up at E. Slide needle from right to left through cross stitch, *not* through material. 4) Go down at F, come up at G. Repeat 3 & 4. 5) To obtain a smooth braid down the middle, space stitches a needle's width apart.

T RAISED STEM

1) Stitch parallel bars ¼″ apart across area to be filled. 2) Using a blunt needle come up at A and slide under first bar [B to C] holding thread to left of needle. 3) Repeat 2 [D to E] and work to top in this way. 4) Begin each row at the bottom. Continue until the basic bars are covered, but do not crowd stitches.

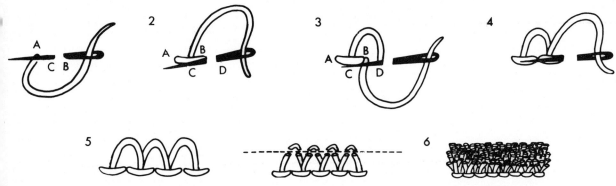

1) Come up at A, go down at B, up at C halfway between A & B. Holding thread below needle, pull tight. 2) With thread above needle, go down at D, up in the same hole as the previous stitch at B. Leave a loop. 3 & 4) Repeat, holding thread first below needle, then above. To keep loops even, measure them over your finger. 5) shows cut and uncut loops. 6) If loops are to be cut, work whole area, then trim.

V BRICK

1) Come up at A, go down at B, up at C, down at D, making a row of even stitches across the shape. 2) Repeat on the next line, coming up halfway between the first row of stitches. 3) Repeat, coming up in the holes made by the previous stitches, forming a brick effect.

W BURDEN

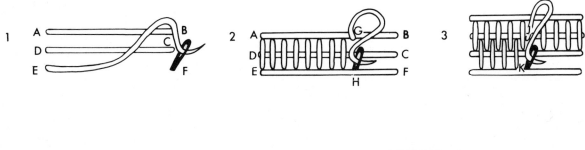

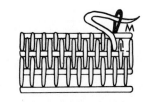

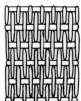

1) Work parallel lines across shape [A to B, C to D, etc.]. 2) Starting in center of shape to keep stitches straight, work a row of stitches across one line, G to H, touching threads above and below. 3 & 4) Repeat 2, fitting the stitches in like Brick Stitch [V]. 5) shows finished effect.

X LAID WORK *tied with criss cross*

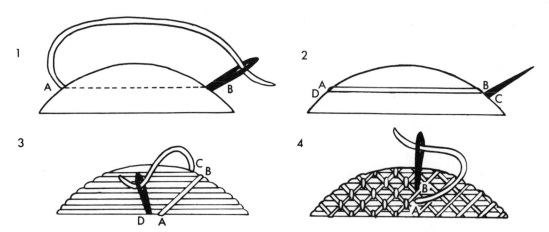

1) Come up at A, go down at B, starting in the center of the shape, to keep stitches straight. 2) Come up at C, close to where you went down at B. Closely fill shape. Only small stitches should appear on the back. 3) To hold stitches flat, work diagonal lines across shape, first in one direction [A to B, C to D], then in the other. Make perfect diamonds. 4) Hold diamonds in position with small straight stitches.

Y LAID WORK *tied with straight lines*

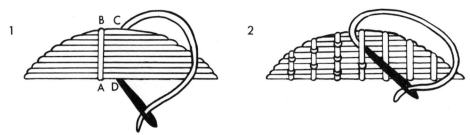

Repeat 1 & 2 of Laid Work [criss cross]. 1) Then hold long stitches flat with horizontal bars [A to B, C to D]. 2) Hold bars firm with small stitches placed alternately.

Z SQUARED FILLING

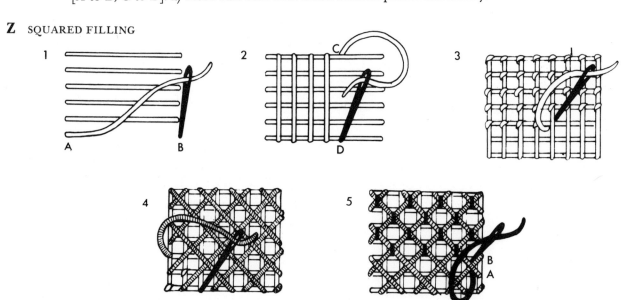

1 & 2) Make a network of perfect squares. 3) Hold this down with slanting stitches at intersections. 4) In contrasting color, cross diagonally every other square in both directions. 5) Hold these stitches down with straight stitches that fit the basic squares.